Romance

Romance

Romance

Romance

Romance

Roman

Presented to

_____

On the occasion of

_____

From

_____

Date

_____

Romance

compiled by
Ellyn Sanna

BARBOUR
PUBLISHING, INC.

Published by Barbour Publishing, Inc., P.O. Box 719, Uhrichsville, Ohio 44683
http://www.barbourbooks.com

 Member of the
Evangelical Christian
Publishers Association

Printed in China.

Romance

Falling In Love

Love is the master key that opens
the gates of happiness.
OLIVER WENDELL HOLMES

Ten Ways to Know You're in Love

1. You find yourself doodling a certain name on business papers and shopping lists.
2. Everything suddenly seems brighter, more exciting, and full of life and color.
3. You miss the other person even though the two of you just talked an hour ago.
4. The person has invaded your dreams.
5. You find yourself wanting to talk about everything together.
6. You like yourself more when you're with the other person.
7. You have everything in common—and at the same time, you're so different from each other that you want to know more and more about the other person.
8. You feel closer to God than you ever have before.
9. You can play together like children.
10. You never get tired of being together.

$\mathcal{L}ove$ is a short word, but it contains all: it means the body, the soul, the life, the entire being. We feel it as we feel the warmth of the blood, we breathe it as we breathe the air, we carry it in ourselves as we carry our thoughts. Nothing more exists for us. It is not a word; it is an inexpressible state indicated by four letters.

GUY DE MAUPASSANT, *OUR HEARTS*

*Love consists in this, that two Solitudes protect
and touch and greet each other.*
RAINER MARIA RILKE

$\mathcal{F}or$ it is a fire that kindling its first embers in the narrow nook of a private bosom, caught from a wandering spark out of another private heart, glows and enlarges until it warms and beams upon multitudes of men and women, upon the universal heart of all, and so lights up the whole world and all nature with its generous flames.

RALPH WALDO EMERSON, *ON LOVE*

Love is my life,
life is my love,
love is my whole
felicity,
Love is my sweet,
sweet is my love,
I am in love,
and love in me.

MICHAEL DRAYTON,
A SHEPHERD'S GARLAND

Love is the most intensive desire of the soul to enjoy beauty, and, where it is reciprocal, is the most entire and exact union of hearts. . . . [Love] gives courage to the most fearful; sharpens the wit of the most simple; gives fidelity to the most depraved minds, constancy to the most unsettled; and, of itself alone, hath power to draw those hearts which have received it to acts of goodness, honesty, virtue, and gallantry, with more efficacy than all the most exact examples of history and philosophy. . . . The desire of a lover is to be loved, and that perfect union of hearts is the perfection of lovers' happiness. . .as love is the cause of the greatest ills that men suffer, it is the cause also of the most perfect pleasures, consisting only in extremes; and as many as are made miserable by love, none are made happy without love.

ALGERNON SIDNEY,
OF LOVE

A Birthday

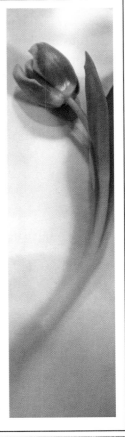

My heart is like a singing bird
 Whose nest is in a watered shoot;
My heart is like an apple tree
 Whose boughs are bent
   with thickest fruit;
My heart is like a rainbow shell
 That paddles in a halcyon sea;
My heart is gladder than all these
 Because my love is come to me.

Raise me a dais of silk and down;
 Hang it with vair and purple dyes;
Carve it in doves, and pomegranates,
 And peacocks with a hundred eyes;
Work it in gold and silver grapes,
 In leaves, and silver fleurs-de-lys;
Because the birthday of my life
 Is come, my love is come to me.

CHRISTINA GEORGINA ROSSETTI

Dear Mary, You will no doubt remind me that we met just a fortnight ago, and I cannot deny that the hours we have spent together have been short. But what quantity we crammed into that brief time! Already I feel that I know you better than I have ever known anyone before. Today as I walked to work I found myself remembering all you had told me about Drusilla, the imaginary horse who was your childhood companion. I realized all at once that a complete stranger was looking at me with a bemused smile as I beamed foolishly into her face. I ducked my head and hurried on my way, but the next second I was reliving the moment when we sat on the gate, watching the moon rise behind your father's barn. Once again, I found I was smiling at strangers, my happiness written across my face for all to see.

When can we see each other again? Please tell me it will be soon.

With sincere affection, I remain,

Your friend, Henry

FROM HENRY PRESTON
TO MARY BROWN, 1922

Shall I compare thee to a summer's day?
Thou art more lovely and more temperate:
Rough winds do shake the darling buds of May,
And summer's lease hath all too short a date:
Sometimes too hot the eye of heaven shines,
And often is his gold complexion dimm'd;
And every fair from fair sometime declines,
By chance or nature's changing course untrimm'd;
But thy eternal summer shall not fade,
Nor lose possession of that fair thou ow'st;
Nor shall Death brag thou wander'st in his shade,
When in eternal lines to time thou grow'st;
So long as men can breathe, or eyes can see,
So long lives this, and this gives life to thee.

WILLIAM SHAKESPEARE

Ah, love, let us be true
To one another! for the world, which seems
To lie before us like a land of dreams,
So various, so beautiful, so new,
Hath really neither joy, nor love, nor light,
Nor certitude, nor peace, nor help for pain;
And we are here as on a darkling plain
Swept with confused alarms of struggle and flight,
Where ignorant armies clash by night.

MATTHEW ARNOLD

Dear God, thank You for this love I feel.
I feel such joy in the world You created;
I am so grateful to be alive. Please bless the one I love.
Amen.

Dost ask (my dear) what service I will have?
To love me day and night is all I crave,
To dream on me, to expect, to think on me,
Depend and hope, still covet me to see,
Delight thyself in me, but wholly mine,
For know, my love, that I am wholly thine.

TERENCE,
THE ANATOMY OF MELANCHOLY
(TRANS. ROBERT BURTON)

Many waters cannot quench love;
rivers cannot wash it away.
SONG OF SOLOMON 8:7 (NIV)

Love is the emblem of eternity: it confounds all notion of time:
effaces all memory of a beginning, all fear of an end.
MADAME DE STAËL

Kisses

And what is a kiss when all is done?
A rosy dot over the "i" of loving. . .
EDMUND ROSTAND,
CYRANO DE BERGERAC

A kiss without a beard
is like an egg without salt.
GERMAN PROVERB

Dear Mac, it was so lovely!
I don't know how to thank you for it in any way
but this." And, drawing down his tall head, she gave
him the birthday kiss she had given all the others.

But this time it produced a singular effect: for Mac turned
scarlet, then grew pale; and when Rose added playfully, thinking to
relieve the shyness of so young a poet, "Never say again you don't
write poetry, or call your verses rubbish: I knew you were a genius,
and now I'm sure of it," he broke out, as if against his will—

"No. It isn't genius: It is love!" Then, as she shrunk a little, star-
tled at his energy, he added, with an effort at self-control which
made his voice sound strange.

"I didn't mean to speak, but I can't suffer you to deceive yourself so. I must tell the truth, and not let you kiss me like a cousin
when I love you with all my heart and soul!"

LOUISA M. ALCOTT,
ROSE IN BLOOM

No, no, the utmost share
Of my desire shall be,
Only to kiss the air
That lately kissed thee.

ROBERT HERRICK

The kiss that ends the wedding ceremony is an ancient tradition that is widely considered to mark the beginning of married life. In some countries this kiss was even made part of the laws, probably the only ceremonial kiss to ever receive legal sanction.

A loving kiss is. . .

- sweeter than chocolate.
- as joyful as Christmas.
- more expressive than all the fancy poems in any book.
- more exciting than a roller coaster ride.
- worth more than gold or silver.

A kiss may indeed be washed away,
but the fire in the heart cannot be quenched.

GERMAN PROVERB

*The kiss is a fruit which one
ought to pluck from the tree itself.*

FRENCH PROVERB

A Danish couple decided to break off their engagement:
"It is best, I suppose, that we return each other's letters?" said he.
"I think so too," replied she, "but shall we not at the same time
give each other all our kisses back?" They did so, and thus agreed
to renew their engagement.

Love's Philosophy

The fountains mingle with the river
And the rivers with ocean,
The winds of heaven mix forever
With a sweet emotion;
Nothing in the world is single,
All things by a law divine
In one another's being mingle—
Why not I with thine?

See the mountains kiss high heaven,
And the waves clasp one another;
No sister-flower would be forgiven
If it disdain'd its brother:
And the sunlight clasps the earth,
And the moonbeams kiss the sea—
What are all these kissings worth,
If thou kiss not me?

PERCY BYSSHE SHELLEY

Dear Mary, Who would have thought that the spot where Main Street crosses Willow Creek would become such an important place? Do you think they will put up a monument? "Here in this spot Henry Preston did kiss Mary Brown for the very first time on the 3rd day of May in 1922." The moment was certainly momentous enough to merit a bronze plaque. I trembled so you may have thought there was an earthquake, but let me confess, it was only my heart shaking with fear and joy.

Of course if I have my way, the town will soon be quite sprinkled with similar bronze plaques. . .

FROM HENRY PRESTON
TO MARY BROWN, 1922

Dear God,
thank You
for giving us
so many ways
to express our love.
Amen.

Let him kiss me with the kisses of his mouth: for thy love is better than wine.
SONG OF SOLOMON 1:2 (KJV)

The measure of one's devotion is doing, not merely saying.
Love is demonstration, not merely saying.
Love is demonstration, not merely declaration.

<small>ANONYMOUS</small>

Give thy heart's best treasure,
And the more thou spendest
From thy little store,
With a double bounty,
God will give thee more.

<small>ADELAIDE A. PROCTOR</small>

Nothing is sweeter than love, nothing higher,
nothing broader, nothing better, either in heaven or earth;
because love is born of God.

<small>THOMAS Á KEMPIS</small>

When We're Apart

Love reckons hours for months,
and days for years; and every little absence is an age.
JOHN DRYDEN

When you're apart from the one you love. . .

- the hours seem like days.
- you can't sleep at night.
- when you do sleep, you dream about your love.
- every little thing that happens,
    both good and bad,
        just makes you miss your love still more.
- you can't think of anything else.
- you count the days until you can be together again.

We arrived here last night at twelve o'clock, and it is now before breakfast the next morning. I can of course tell you nothing of the future, and though I shall not close this letter till post-time, yet I do not know exactly when that is. Yet, if you are still very impatient, look along the letter, and you will see another date, when I may have something to relate. . . . Well, but the time presses. I am now going to the banker's to send you money for your journey, which I shall address to you at Florence, Post Office. Pray come instantly to Este, where I shall be waiting in the utmost anxiety for your arrival.

Do you know, dearest, how this letter was written? By scrap and patches and interrupted every minute. The gondola is now coming to take me to the banker's. Este is a little place and the house found without difficulty. I shall count four days for this letter, one day for packing, four for coming here–and the ninth or tenth day we shall meet.

I am too late for the post, but I send an express to overtake it. Enclosed is an order for fifty pounds. If you knew all that I have to do! Dearest love, be well, be happy, come to me. Confide in your own constant and affectionate

P.B.S: Kiss the blue-eyed darlings for me, and do not let William forget me. Clara cannot recollect me.

FROM PERCY BYSSHE SHELLEY
TO MARY GODWIN SHELLEY
BAGNI DI LUCCA,
SUNDAY MORNING, 23RD AUGUST, 1818

Love Song

The honey of the Hybla bees
Is not so sweet as kissing you;
Nor autumn wind in dying trees
So wistful is as missing you.

And when you are not mine to kiss,
My every thought is haunting you,
And when your mouth is mine, I miss
The wistfulness of wanting you.

SAMUEL HOFFENSTEIN

Dear God, be with my love when we can't be together. You know how empty I feel without my love. . .remind me that You are my first love, my best love, and nothing will ever separate me from Your love. Amen.

Wonderful Boy,

Where are you tonight? Your letter came only an hour ago—cruel hour—I had hoped you would spend it with me here.

Paris is a morgue without you: before I knew you, it was Paris, and I thought it heaven; but now it is a vast desert of desolation and loneliness. It is like the face of a clock, bereft of hands.

All the pictures that hung in my memory before I knew you have faded and given place to our radiant moments together.

Now I cannot live apart from you; your words, even though bitter, dispel all the cares of the world and make me happy; my art has been suckled by them and softly rocked in their tender cradle; they are as necessary to me now as sunlight and air.

I am hungry for them as for food, I am thirsty for them, and my thirst is overwhelming. Your words are my food, your breath is my wine. You are everything to me.

FROM SARAH BERNHARDT
TO VICTORIEN SARDOU

Finding a Lifelong Love

Committing ourselves for a lifetime takes courage.
Love is a road we walk, around bends and up hills,
through delightful valleys and across long deserts,
and we cannot know where this road will lead us in the end.
We do not know the future—but our faith in God
and one another makes us step out unafraid.
We do not walk alone along this road,
for Christ goes with us all the way.

Rose, am I getting on a little? Does a hint of fame help me nearer to the prize I'm working for? Is your heart more willing to be won?"

He did not stir a step, but looked at her with such intense longing that his glance seemed to draw her nearer like an irresistible appeal; for she went and stood before him, holding out both hands, as if she offered all her little store, as she said with simplest sincerity,

"It is not worth so much beautiful endeavor; but, if you still want so poor a thing, it is yours."

He caught the hands in his, and seemed about to take the rest of her, but hesitated for an instant, unable to believe that so much happiness was true.

"Are you sure, Rose, very sure? Don't let a momentary admiration blind you: I'm not a poet yet; and the best are but mortal men, you know."

"It is not admiration, Mac."

"Nor gratitude for the small share I've taken in saving Uncle? I had a

> *Beloved, let us love one another: for love is of God; and every one that loveth is born of God, and knoweth God.*
>
> 1 JOHN 4:7 (KJV)

debt to pay, as well as Phebe, and was as glad to risk my life."

"No, it is not gratitude."

"Nor pity for my patience? I've only done a little yet, and am as far as ever from being like your hero. I can work and wait still longer, if you are not sure; for I must have all or nothing."

"O Mac! why will you be so doubtful? You said you'd make me love you, and you've done it. Will you believe me now?" And, with a sort of desperation, she threw herself into his arms, clinging there in eloquent silence, while he held her close; feeling, with a thrill of tender triumph, that this was no longer little Rose, but a loving woman, ready to live and die for him.

LOUISA M. ALCOTT,
ROSE IN BLOOM

Love me for love's sake, that evermore thou may'st love on through love's eternity.

ELIZABETH
BARRETT BROWNING

> *How can
> we be troubled
> about
> the future road,
> since it belongs
> to Thee?
> How can
> we be troubled
> where it leads,
> since it finally
> but leads
> us to Thee!*
> JOHN HENRY NEWMAN

All the wonderful old love stories tell of that moment when the hero and heroine dare commit themselves to a forever love. . .

"*I have* a dream," he said slowly. "I persist in dreaming it, although it has often seemed to me that it could never come true. I dream of a home with a hearth-fire in it, a cat and dog, the footsteps of friends—and you!"

Anne wanted to speak but she could find no words. Happiness was breaking over her like a wave. It almost frightened her.

"I asked you a question over two years ago, Anne. If I ask it again today will you give me a different answer?"

Still Anne could not speak. But she lifted her eyes, shining with all the love-rapture of countless generations, and looked into his for a moment. He wanted no other answer.

L. M. MONTGOMERY,
ANNE OF THE ISLAND

Yesterday I felt better than I have done since the accident. I ran about the house quite cheerily, for me. I wanted to see Mother for something and flew singing into the parlor, where I had left her shortly before. But she was not there, and Dr. Elliott was. I started back and was about to leave the room, but he detained me.

"Come in, I beg of you," he said. "Let us put a stop to this."

"To what?" I asked, looking up into his face.

"To your evident terror of being alone with me, of hearing me speak. Let me assure you, once for all, that nothing would tempt me to annoy you by urging myself upon you, as you seem to fear I may be tempted to do. I cannot force you to love me nor would I if I could. If you ever want a friend, you will find one in me. But do not think of me as your lover or treat me as if I were always lying in wait for a chance to remind you of it. That I shall never do, never."

"Oh, no, of course not!" I broke forth, my face all in a glow and tears of mortification raining down my cheeks. "I knew you did not care for me! I knew you had got over it!"

I don't know which of us began it, I don't think he did and I am sure I did not, but the next moment I was folded all up in his great long arms, and a new life had begun!

MRS. E. PRENTISS,
STEPPING HEAVENWARD

Yes, it's late, and I'm so tired." Jo's voice was more pathetic than she knew; for now the sun seemed to have gone in as suddenly as it came out, the world grew muddy and miserable again, and for the first time she discovered that her feet were cold, her head ached, and that her heart was colder than the former, fuller of pain than the latter. Mr. Bhaer was going away. He only cared for her as a friend; it was all a mistake, and the sooner it was over the better. With this idea in her head, she hailed an approaching omnibus with such a hasty gesture that the daisies flew out of the pot and were badly damaged.

"This is not our omniboos," said the Professor, waving the loaded vehicle away and stopping to pick up the poor little flowers.

"I beg you pardon, I didn't see the name distinctly. Never mind, I can walk. I'm used to plodding in the mud," returned Jo, winking hard because she would have died rather than openly wipe her eyes.

Mr. Bhaer saw the drops on her cheeks, though she turned her head away. The sight seemed to touch him very much, for, suddenly stooping down, he asked in a tone that meant a great deal: "Heart's dearest, why do you cry?"

Now if Jo had not been new to this sort of thing she would have said she wasn't crying, had a cold in her head, or told any other feminine fib proper to the occasion; instead of which that undignified creature answered, with an irrepressible sob:

"Because you are going away."

"Ach, that is so good!" cried Mr. Bhaer, managing to clasp his hands in spite of the umbrella and the bundles. "Jo, I haf nothing but much love to gif you. I came to see if you could care for it, and I waited to be sure that I was something more than a friend. Am I? Can you make a little place in your heart for old Fritz?" he added, all in one breath.

"Oh yes!" said Jo, and he was quite satisfied, for she folded both hands over his arm, and looked up at him with an expression that plainly showed how happy she would be to walk through life beside him, even though she had no better shelter than the old umbrella, if he carried it.

LOUISA M. ALCOTT, LITTLE WOMEN

I suppose, Anne, you must think it's funny I should like Fred so well when he's so different from the kind of man I've always said I would marry. . .the tall, slender kind? But somehow I wouldn't want Fred to be tall and slender. . .because, don't you see, he wouldn't be Fred then. Of course," added Diana rather dolefully, "we will be a dreadfully pudgy couple. But after all that's better than one of us being short and fat and the other tall and lean."

L. M. MONTGOMERY,
ANNE OF AVONLEA

"Oh, of course there's a risk in marrying anybody,"
conceded Charlotta the Fourth,
"but, when all's said and done, Miss Shirley, ma'am,
there's many a worse thing than a husband."

L. M. MONTGOMERY,
ANNE OF AVONLEA

Dear God,

I can't help but feel a little scared
now that I've committed myself
to loving this person forever.
What if I change?
What if we both change?
How can we know our love will last?
Jesus, we're counting on
Your strength to carry us
when we falter. We're relying on
Your love that never fails. Amen.

Yes, marriage is a great risk—it's a plunge into the deep. But the greater the risk we take on God, the deeper and farther we dare to go from the safe shore, the richer shall be the treasures we will find and the greater the delights.

INGRID TROBISCH,
ON OUR WAY REJOICING

White Lace and Promises

Place me like a seal over your heart,
   like a seal over your arm;
for love is as strong as death. . . .
It burns like a blazing fire,
   like a mighty flame.

SONG OF SOLOMON 8:6 (NIV)

Ten Romantic Places to Go with the One I Love

1. A quaint bed-and-breakfast in the middle of nowhere (the library will have a directory)
2. A four-star hotel in the center of a big city (like the Plaza in New York)
3. A long, empty beach (like Plum Island in Massachusetts or the Outer Banks in North Carolina)
4. A ski lodge in Vermont or Colorado
5. A cabin in the woods (a state park maybe)
6. An ocean cruise (freighters are just as romantic and cost less)
7. Somewhere that time's stood still (like Williamsburg, Virginia or Quebec City in Canada)
8. Paris (let's go ahead and dream— anything's possible)
9. Niagara Falls (the traditional spot for honeymooners)
10. Anywhere the two of us can spend time alone

There is no more lovely,
friendly, and charming
relationship, communion,
or company than a
good marriage.

MARTIN LUTHER

I will make you brooches and toys for your delight
Of bird-song at morning and star-shine at night.
I will make a palace fit for you and me,
Of green days in forests and blue days at sea.

ROBERT LOUIS STEVENSON

I must write you a line or two and see if that will assist in dismissing you from my mind for ever so short a time. Upon my soul I can thing of nothing else. . . . I am forgetful of everything but seeing you again—my life seems to stop there—I see no further. You have absorbed me. I have a sensation at the present moment as though I was dissolving—I should be exquisitely miserable without the hope of soon seeing you. I should be afraid to separate myself far from you. My sweet Fanny, will your heart never change? My love, will it? I have no limit now to my love. . . .

FROM JOHN KEATS
TO FANNY BRAWNE, 1818

Lord, I am not worthy
of so good a husband;
but help us both to observe
the holiness of wedded life,
so that we may eternally
abide together near Thee.
ELIZABETH OF HUNGARY, 1207–1231

Dear one, my heart feels as though it might burst with joy, so glad I am to be one with you. You lie there sleeping, just three feet from my chair, and I can scarce believe you're real. Perhaps I'll wake soon and find that you and all we've shared are just a pretty dream.

But no, I stretch out my hand and touch you, feel you warm and solid. Thank God, thank God.

I promise, my love, to be true to you always. I know this is just the beginning of our life; I know we cannot know what will come next, a year down the road, ten years, fifty years. But I trust the future to God, to you, to our love. Whatever comes, I will only love you more.

I picked up this pen only to write a note to say I've gone out for coffee and rolls. If you wake and find me gone, I shall be back immediately. But once I put the pen to paper, I found I could not keep the words of love from rolling out of me, like a river at springtime filled to overflowing with water.

That is how I feel, filled to overflowing with love and life, and all because of you. But if one day, the river should run dry, still, my love, believe me: I will be true.

FROM HENRY PRESTON
TO HIS WIFE MARY, 1924

Doubt that the stars are fire;
　　Doubt that the sun doth move,
Doubt truth to be a liar;
　　But never doubt I love.

WILLIAM SHAKESPEARE,
HAMLET

Love should be essentially an act of the will. . . .
It is a decision. . .it is a promise.
ERICH FROMM

For you have heard my vows, O God. . . .
Then will I ever sing praise to your name
and fulfill my vows day after day.

PSALM 61:5, 8 (NIV)

Dear God, as we begin
our married life together, please be
present with us. We ask You to help
us keep the promises we've made
to one another. Thank You for the
joy and love You've given us. May
Your Spirit always be with us.
Amen.

Forever Lovers

Love's mysteries in souls do grow
And yet the body is his book.

JOHN DONNE

Ten Ways to Say "I Love You"

1. Surprise your love with flowers.
2. Put it in writing.
3. Schedule a getaway weekend for the two of you.
4. Listen to the other person's dreams.
5. Surprise your spouse by going out and getting a little piece of those dreams.
6. Make a habit of saying the words "I love you" every chance you get.
7. Serve your love's favorite foods.
8. Take a nap together.
9. Do each other's chores.
10. Pay attention to the things that please your love the most —and then do them!

How do I love thee? Let me count the ways.
I love thee to the depth and breadth and height
My soul can reach, when feeling out of sight
For the ends of Being and ideal Grace.
I love thee to the level of every day's
Most quiet need, by sun and candlelight.
I love thee freely, as men strive for Right;
I love thee purely, as men turn from Praise.
I love thee with the passion put to use
In my old griefs, and with my childhood's faith.
I love thee with a love I seemed to lose
With my lost saints, I love thee with the breath,
Smiles, tears, of all my life! and, if God choose,
I shall but love thee better after death.

ELIZABETH BARRETT BROWNING

*Love vanquishes time. To lovers, a moment can be eternity,
eternity can be the tick of a clock.*
MARY PARRISH, *ALL THE LOVE IN THE WORLD*

It is a fusion of two hearts—the union of two lives—
the coming together of two tributaries,
which after being joined in marriage,
will flow in the same channel in the same direction. . .
carrying the same burdens
of responsibility and obligation.

PETER MARSHALL

Characteristic of love is its tenderness. . . .
In love hands don't take, grasp, or hold. They caress.
Caressing is the possibility of human hands to be tender.
The careful touch of the hand makes for growth.
Like a gardener who carefully touches the flowers
to enable the light to shine through and stimulate growth,
the hand of the lover allows for the full self-expression of the other.
In love the mouth does not bite, devour, or destroy.
It kisses.

HENRI J. M. NOUWEN,
INTIMACY

If ever two were one, then surely we.
If ever man were loved by wife, then thee;
If ever wife was happy in a man,
Compare with me women if you can.
I prize thy love more than whole mines of gold,
Or all the riches that the East doth hold.
My love is such that rivers cannot quench,
Nor ought but love from thee give recompense.
Thy love is such I can no way repay;
The heavens reward thee manifold, I pray.
Then while we live, in love let's so persevere,
That when we live no more we may love better.

FROM ANNE BRADSTREET
TO HER HUSBAND, 1678

*Love must be learned,
and learned again
and again;
there is no end to it.*
KATHERINE ANNE PORTER

Dear one, remember the time on our honeymoon when we raced to see who could get to the bed first? We both jumped at the same time, and that solid wood bed collapsed under our combined weight. All these years into our marriage, I suspect we should not be surprised if our marriage bed collapses from time to time. After all, the combined weight of our two lives can become rather cumbersome. But just recall, love: We only needed laughter and patience to get our honeymoon bed back in service, and I suspect we shall find the same is true today. And who can tell? I should not be in the least surprised if the reconstructed version gives us even more pleasure and delight than it did before.

FROM HENRY PRESTON
TO HIS WIFE, 1930

Love is not lust, and lust is not love.
Love, if it is anything at all,
is respect; and when respect
for the other's dignity and integrity
is thrown aside, love
folds up like a punctured balloon.

BILLY GRAHAM

Like the sun, love radiates
and warms into life all that it touches.
O. S. MARDEN

Only in a marriage—a marriage where love is—can sex develop into the delightfully positive force God meant it to be. Here is where the excitement of sex really is. When a man and a woman make a lifelong commitment to love and cherish each other, they are giving themselves the time they will need to dismantle the barriers of restraint, shyness, defensiveness, and selfishness that exist between all human beings. It cannot be done in a night or with a rush of passion. It takes time to know and be known.

COLLEEN TOWNSEND EVANS,
A NEW JOY

It is not enough to love those who are near and dear to us.
We must show them that we do so.
LORD AVEBURY

The Christian idea of marriage is based on Christ's words that a man and wife are to be regarded as a single organism—for that is what the words "one flesh" would be in modern English. And the Christians believe that when He said this He was not expressing a sentiment but stating a fact—just as one is stating a fact when one says that a lock and its key are one mechanism, or that a violin and a bow are one musical instrument. The inventor of the human machine was telling us that its two halves, the male and the female, were meant to be combined together in pairs, not simply on the sexual level, but totally combined.

C. S. LEWIS,
MERE CHRISTIANITY

Men marry what they need. I marry you,
morning by morning, day by day, night by night,
and every marriage makes this marriage new.
JOHN CIARDI,
I MARRY YOU

Where the flesh is one, one also is the spirit. Together we pray, husband and wife, together perform our fasts, mutually teaching, exhorting, sustaining. Equally we are found in the church of God, equally at the banquet of God, equally in trials and in refreshments.

FROM TERTULLIAN TO HIS WIFE, CA. 206

Love is the emblem of eternity; it confounds all notion of time; effaces all memory of a beginning, all fear of an end.

MADAME DE STAËL

Dear God, thank You for this love You've given us, and thank You for the delight it brings to us. Thank You for this wonderful gift with which You've blessed our lives. Remind us never to take it for granted, but to give our love the care and attention we would give to anything that is precious to us. Teach us new ways to please each other so that our love may grow day by day and year by year. Amen.

Companions on Life's Road

Don't urge me to leave you or to turn back from you.
Where you go I will go, and where you stay I will stay.
Your people will be my people and your God my God.
Where you die I will die, and there I will be buried.
May the Lord deal with me, be it ever so severely,
if anything but death separates you and me.

RUTH 1:16–17 (NIV)

You are my companion
Down the silver road,
Still and many-changing,
Infinitely changing,
  You are my companion.

  Something sings in lives—
  Days of walking on and on—
  Deep beyond all singing,
  Wonderful past singing.

  This more wonderful—
  We are here together,
  I am your companion.
  You are my companion,
  My own true companion.

EDITH FRANKLIN WYATT

Ten Romantic Songs to Listen to with the One I Love

1. "Have I Told You Lately" by Van Morrison
2. "Unforgettable" by Nat King Cole
3. "Somewhere" from *West Side Story*
4. "We've Only Just Begun" by the Carpenters
5. "When I Fall in Love" by Nat King Cole, Clive Griffen, Celine Dion, and Johnny Matthis
6. "All of Me" by John Pizzarelli
7. "Dream a Little Dream of Me" by Louis Armstrong
8. "Always on My Mind" by Willie Nelson
9. "Woman" by John Lennon
10. "Today" by Jefferson Airplane

Love doesn't make the world go 'round.
Love is what makes the ride worthwhile.
FRANKLIN P. JONES

> *The goal in marriage is not to think alike, but to think together.*
> ROBERT C. DODDS

Love asks for a total disarmament. The encounter in love is an encounter without weapons. . . . We are very able to hide our guns and knives even in the most intimate relationship. An old bitter memory, a slight suspicion about motives, or a small doubt can be as sharp as a knife held behind our back as weapon for defense in case of attack. . . . Are man and woman able to exclude the power in their relationship and become totally available for each other? When the soldier sits down to eat he lays down his weapons, because eating means peace and rest. When he stretches out his body to sleep he is more vulnerable than ever. Table and bed are the two places of intimacy where love can manifest itself in weakness. In love men and women take off all the forms of power, embracing each other in total disarmament.

. . .Love means openness, vulnerability, availability, and confession.

HENRI J. M. NOUWEN,
INTIMACY

*Married life. . .isn't a time for settling down
but for growth, for doing new things.
With each passing year a growing couple will actively look
for new and different things they can do together.*

DALE EVANS ROGERS,
GOD IN THE HARD TIMES

My one and only Josephine, apart from you there is no joy; away from you the world is a desert where I am alone and cannot open my heart. You have taken more than my soul; you are the one thought of my life. When I am tired of the worry of work, when I fear the outcome, when men annoy me. . .I put my hand on my heart; your portrait hangs there, I look at it, and love brings me perfect happiness. . . . Oh, my adorable wife! I don't know what fate has in store for me, but if it keeps me apart from you any longer, it will be unbearable! My courage is not enough for that.

Come and join me; before we die let us at least be able to say: "We had so many happy days!"

FROM NAPOLEON BONAPARTE
TO JOSEPHINE, 1810

*Love does not consist
in gazing at each other
but in looking outward together
in the same direction.*
ANTOINE DE SAINT-EXUPÉRY

Husband and wife must love each other unconditionally, must give each other room to grow, must wait for the infinite reaches of their personality to flower. Each must take the other by the hand along an unglimpsed road, developing the undreamed of potential of that other being. That is the power you have over each other and, in exercising it, you will know that you are one.

LOUIS EVELY,
LOVERS IN MARRIAGE

*We are each of us angels with only one wing.
And we can only fly embracing each other.*
LUCIANO DE CRESCENZO

My love, I feel slightly foolish confessing how much I miss you. After all, you have only been gone not quite twenty-four hours. Only now, though, do I realize how much I have come to depend upon your companionship. Going to the grocer is amusing when you are with me, chopping firewood gives me more pleasure when I know you are applauding my efforts, and all the small, household chores have meaning simply because we do them side by side.

How empty the house seemed tonight when I returned home—dark and cold and lonely. Eating my supper alone, my heart longed for your company. Oh my love, my best companion, how I miss you!

FROM HENRY PRESTON
TO HIS WIFE, 1941

Dear God, I am so grateful to You for giving me a companion on my life's road. Teach us how to walk together. If one stumbles, give us strength to help the other up. When my beloved gets ahead of me, help me to hurry to catch up—and when my beloved falls behind, remind me to wait patiently until we walk hand in hand together once more. Thank You that I do not walk my road alone. Amen.

Best Friends

Can two people walk together
without agreeing on the direction?
AMOS 3:3 (NLT)

Two hearts, two lives
Joined together in friendship
United forever in love.

The Heart's Anchor

Think of me as your friend, I pray,
And call me by a loving name;
I will not care what others say,
If only you will remain the same.
I will not care how dark the night,
I will not care how wild the storm,
Your love will fill my heart with light
An shield me close and keep me warm.

WILLIAM WINTER

Ten Little Ways
to Express My Appreciation
to the One I Love

1. Write a love note and put it in a lunch bag or suitcase.
2. Serve my love breakfast in bed.
3. Give my love a back rub.
4. Write a love note on the bathroom mirror.
5. Go see a movie I don't really want to see—but my love does.
6. Surprise my love with a cold drink on a hot day— or a warm one on a cold day.
7. Remember to say thank you for even routine chores.
8. Express my appreciation for my love's physical appearance.
9. Clean off the car in the winter and warm it up before my love goes to work in the morning.
10. Never criticize my love to others.

What a thing friendship is—world without end!
ROBERT BROWNING

Knowing is the most profound kind of love,
giving someone the gift of knowledge about yourself.

MARSHA NORMAN

The movement into marriage involves the risks of intimacy. In marriage I must be able to come close to you in a way that lets you know and influence me. I must face the risk of being changed, of coming to a different awareness of who I am, as a result of our life together. I must accept the responsibility of my own influence in your life as well. Intimacy involves an overlapping of space, a willingness to be influenced, an openness to the possibility of change. It invites me beyond myself.

EVELYN AND JAMES WHITEHEAD,
MARRYING WELL

Dear Mary, Sometimes you are so different from myself that you startle me. For instance, my love, how can it be that I have lived all these years with a woman who insists on drinking sugar in her coffee? And then you must know I still have not quite forgiven you for favoring Hoover over Roosevelt.

No, love, I must confess, when I look at you I certainly don't see my mirror image.

But who would want to? I have a shaving mirror that provides me with an accurate reflection quite nicely, thank you. You are much more interesting this way, my love, much more fascinating. We may argue fiercely every day at least once before bedtime, but I doubt I shall ever grow bored.

And still and all, my Mary, despite our differences, I have never had a friend as close as you, as trusted and beloved.

FROM HENRY PRESTON
TO HIS WIFE MARY, 1935

Tenderness emerges from the fact that two persons, longing, as all individuals do, to overcome the separateness and isolation to which we are all heir because we are individuals, can participate in a relationship that, for the moment, is not of two isolated selves but a union.

ROLLO MAY

However rare true love is,
true friendship is rarer.
LA ROCHEFOUCAULD

Believe this: I accept you. I know you little and I know you much, but whichever way it goes, I accept you. Your manhood comes through in a thousand ways, rare and wonderful. I accept you. . . .

What an awesome thing it is to feel oneself on the verge of the possibility of really knowing another person. . . . Getting to know someone, entering that new world, is an ultimate, irretrievable leap into the unknown. . . . We recognize each other. And having recognized each other, is it any wonder that our souls hold hands and cling together even while our minds equivocate, hesitate, vacillate, and tremble?

TO ELDRIDGE CLEAVER,
TWENTIETH CENTURY

The greatest happiness of life is the conviction
that we are loved, loved for ourselves,
or rather loved in spite of ourselves.
VICTOR HUGO

Dear God, thank You that my love is also my best friend.
Sometimes we seem so different—and yet I know that our love and
commitment to each other means that we can always count on
each other, share everything, and learn from each other. Teach us
to enjoy our differences and celebrate the unique qualities that
make our life together always exciting, never boring. I am so grateful for this special best friend You've given me. Help me to show
my love how much I appreciate the friendship we share. Amen.

Let us stop just saying we love each other;
let us really show it by our actions.
1 JOHN 3:18 (NLT)

For Better, For Worse
Going Further Down Love's Road

Be humble and gentle. Be patient with each other,
making allowance for each other's faults because of your love.
Always keep yourselves united in the Holy Spirit,
and bind yourselves together with peace.

Ephesians 4:2–3 (NLT)

Grow old along with me!
The best is yet to be,
The last of life, for which the first was made.

ROBERT BROWNING

Ten Ways to Add Romance to Your Life

1. Eat with music playing.
2. Light candles.
3. Redecorate your bedroom.
4. Take a walk in the moonlight.
5. Go "parking" in the country.
6. Go for a hansom cab ride.
7. Rent a romantic movie and curl up together to watch it.
8. Meet for lunch—and make plans for your evening.
9. Rent a canoe and bring a picnic.
10. Hold hands.

At the top of the list
[of what makes a successful marriage],
I think, is a sense of humor.

DEBORAH KERR

We don't naturally grow together and love each other more. We tend to grow apart, to grow distant. So we have to work hard at marriage. It's the most fun work in the world, but still it's work.

ANNE ORTLUND

It is not true
that love makes
all things easy;
it makes us choose
what is difficult.

GEORGE ELIOT

Our relations with one another are like a stone arch,
which would collapse if the stones did not mutually support
each other, and which is upheld in this very way.

SENECA

It is good to have a healthy honesty on the part of those married longer years, as they relate that awful moment of anger when the wedding ring was thrown on the floor and rolled into a crack and took two hours to find and put back on. It is good for the ones married just a short time to know that a marriage can weather "down" moments and rough places, as well as coming to know that it is important to work at relationships.

EDITH SCHAEFFER,
WHAT IS A FAMILY?

We don't love qualities,
we love a person;
sometimes by reason
of their defects
as well as their qualities.

JACQUES MARITAIN

Fidelity is the virtue at the core of the lifelong commitment of marriage. In the phrase "lifelong commitment" we begin to glimpse the complexity of this virtue: Commitment suggests stability and lifelong implies change. . . . Marital fidelity combines commitment and change as two persons seek to grow in the same direction; fidelity is the careful tending of both the commitments and the changes necessary in a maturing love.

EVELYN AND JAMES WHITEHEAD,
MARRYING WELL

*Love is an act of endless forgiveness,
a tender look which becomes a habit.*
PETER USTINOV

My love for Heathcliff resembles the eternal rocks beneath—a source of little visible delight, but necessary. Nelly, I am Heathcliff—he's always, always in my mind—not as a pleasure, any more than I am always a pleasure to myself—but, as my own being."

EMILY BRONTË, *WUTHERING HEIGHTS*

If couples would put
half the effort into marriage
that they put into courtship,
they would be surprised
how things would brighten up.

BILLY GRAHAM

When you are old and grey and full of sleep,
And nodding by the fire, take down this book,
And slowly read, and dream of the soft look
Your eyes had once, and of their shadows deep;
How many loved your moments of glad grace,
And loved your beauty, with false love or true,
But one man loved the pilgrim soul in you,
And loved the sorrows of your changing face.

WILLIAM BUTLER YEATS

Oh, no–not ev'n when
first we lov'd
Wert thou as dear as
   now thou art;
Thy beauty then my senses mov'd.
But now thy virtues bind my heart.
What was but Passion's sign before
Has since been turn'd to Reason's vow;
And, though I then might
   love thee more,
Trust me, I love thee better now.

Although my heart in earlier youth
Might kindle with more wild desire,
Believe me, it has gain'd in truth
Much more than it has lost in fire.
The flame now warms my inmost core
That then but sparkled o'er my brow,
And though I seem'd to love thee more,
Yet, oh, I love thee better now.

THOMAS MOORE

Love is the river of life in this world. Think not that ye know it who stand at the little tinkling rill, the first small fountain.

   Not until you have gone through the rocky gorges and not lost the stream; not until you have gone through the meadow, and the stream has widened and deepened until fleets could ride on its bosom; not until beyond the meadow you have come to the unfathomable ocean, and poured your treasure into its depths—not until then can you know what love is.

HENRY WARD BEECHER

*Since nothing we intend is ever faultless,
and nothing we attempt ever without error,
and nothing we achieve without some measure
of finitude and fallibility we call humanness,
we are saved by forgiveness.*
DAVID AUGSBERGER

We are not united for the sake of sharing with each other only that which gives pleasure; but that you may pour out your heart at all times to me and I to you, whatever it may contain; that I must and will bear your sorrows, your thoughts, your naughtinesses, if you have any, and love you as you are—not as you ought to be or might be. Make me serviceable. . .I am there for that purpose, at your disposal; but never be embarrassed in any way with me. Trust me unreservedly in the conviction that I accept everything that comes from you with profound love.

FROM BISMARCK TO JOANNA,
NINETEENTH CENTURY

If we spend our lives in loving, we have no leisure to complain, or to feel unhappiness.
JOSEPH JOUBERT

Disregarding another person's faults preserves love.
PROVERBS 17:9 (NLT)

An Angel That Bears a Sword

I've been thinking a lot about marriage lately. I realized that I've always thought finding someone to love me would be like the end of the love story. . .and then we'd live happily ever after. It's occurred to me that that's just the beginning. Then the hard part comes, the real work. I've always looked at marriage as something for me, something that will make me feel happy and secure and loved. But that's pretty selfish." He leaned forward, his elbows on his knees. "I always thought, you know, that if I died to myself, the way Jesus talked about, then I'd be able to give up the desire to be married. For Christ, you know. Like what Christ said in John twelve, verse twenty-five: 'The man who loves his life will lose it, while the man who hates his life in this world will keep it for eternal life.' But it's occurred to me that God might want me to marry, not just to make me happy, but to teach me to give up my life so that I can keep it for eternal life. And that will hurt of course, because dying to my self always does. Not that it's not worth it in the end. But I think marriage will be an angel that bears a sword."

RAE SIMONS, *THE REFUGE*

Believe me if all those endearing young charms,
Which I gaze on so fondly today.
Were to change by tomorrow and flee from my arms;
Like the fairy gifts fading away,

Thou wouldst still be adored, as this moment thou art,
Let thy loveliness fade as it will,
And around the dear ruin, each wish of my heart,
Would entwine itself verdantly still.

It is not while beauty and youth are thy own,
And thy cheeks unprofaned by a tear,
That the fervor and faith of a soul may be known,
To which time will but make thee more dear!

No, the heart that has truly loved never forgets,
But as truly loves on to the close,
As the sunflower turns to her god when he sets
The same look which she turned when he rose!

THOMAS MOORE

Enduring Love

Those wispy clouds look like someone streaked the sky with red and orange paint," the young woman said.

The young man smiled and tasted the salty air. He smoothed the mounds of sand beneath the blanket.

"I love you," he said. He held her in his arms and caressed her face. "Will you marry me?" He gave her a black velvet box.

"Yes," she answered and opened the box. He placed the ring on her left hand, and her eyes sparkled like the blue diamond.

"I have found favor in the eyes of the Lord," he said, "so I will call you Grace."

Throughout their marriage, the couple kept their romance alive. He knew she enjoyed gifts, so he surprised her with presents. They were simple gifts wrapped in pretty paper and ribbons. She treasured these tokens of his love.

"You are always faithful," she said, "and so I'll call you Noah."

Grace honored her husband with simple acts of kindness. She

started the fire before he came home from a long day at the factory. She shoveled the driveway. She weeded the garden.

"I feel like a king," he said.

They transformed their simple house into a cozy home. Noah carved figurines for the corner hutch. Grace embroidered wall hangings and sewed quilts. Their favorite quilt covered their bed with a pattern of violet and white phlox, like the wild flowers Noah picked for Grace one special weekend.

Just like the quilt's flowery center square, they framed their love in memories. They held hands and prayed together.

"Thank You, God, for our enduring love," Grace said.

Noah caressed her face and leaned to kiss her good night.

Their love grew not because of romantic settings or expensive gifts. Instead, it grew from the soil of God's own enduring

When two caring people who are committed to each other wrestle with the inevitable hard times that confront every married couple in the spirit of kindness and tenderness and forgiveness, miracles do happen.

Dale Evans Rogers,
God in the Hard Times

They are like trees planted along the riverbank, bearing fruit each season without fail. Their leaves never wither, and in all they do, they prosper.
PSALM 1:3 (NLT)

love. They chose to put the other's desires first. They spent time together, surprising each other with unexpected gifts and acts of kindness. They kept their expectations simple.

After fifty years, they moved into a new home. Grace pushed Noah's wheelchair down the long corridor. She stopped at the door decorated with an embroidered wall hanging. With his shaky left hand, Noah painstakingly turned the key and opened the door.

"Thank you, Noah," Grace said.

She smoothed out the folds of the quilt on their bed, and her fingers traced the violet and white phlox at the quilt's center. Noah watched her wrinkled hands, and his mouth shaped a crooked smile. The blue diamond sparkled as brightly as it did the summer night he gave it to her.

As so often happened after all these years, their thoughts ran together. "Noah, do you remember the night of our engagement. . . those wispy clouds and the salty air?" Grace asked him.

He nodded and began to cry. Since his stroke, he could no longer speak, but they needed no words to communicate their love. Grace wiped his tears. She fluffed the heart-shaped pillows, then sat on the love seat close to Noah's wheelchair. They held hands and prayed together.

"Thank You, God, for our enduring love," Grace whispered. She caressed Noah's face and leaned to kiss him good night.

DONNA LANGE

Dear God, thank You that You have given us a love that will stand the test of time. We intend to keep our promises to each other, no matter what; we know You will give us the strength to walk our marriage path from beginning to end. Thank You for the joy and laughter, passion and intimacy we have found in our marriage—and thank You too for the heartaches and hurt feelings, the arguments and conflict. Through it all, may we keep our eyes on You, so that our commitment to each other will grow stronger and deeper, a "durable fire" that will never be extinguished. Amen.

True Love
Wears God's Face

Love is patient and kind. Love is not jealous or boastful
or proud or rude. Love does not demand its own way.
Love is not irritable, and it keeps no record of when it has been
wronged. It is never glad about injustice but rejoices
whenever the truth wins out. Love never gives up,
never loses faith, is always hopeful, and endures
through every circumstance. . . .
Let love be your highest goal.
1 CORINTHIANS 13:4–7, 14:1 (NLT)

I would like to have engraved inside every wedding band
BE KIND ONE TO ANOTHER.
This is the Golden Rule of marriage
and the secret of making love last through the years.
RANDOLPH RAY,
MY LITTLE CHURCH AROUND THE CORNER

A good relationship has a pattern like a dance and is built on some of the same rules. . . . When the heart is flooded with love there is no room in it for fear, for doubt, for hesitation. And it is this lack of fear that makes for the dance. When each partner loves so completely that he has forgotten to ask himself whether or not he is loved in return; when he only knows that he loves and is moving to its music—then, and then only, are two people able to dance perfectly in tune to the same rhythm.

ANNE MORROW LINDBERGH,
GIFT FROM THE SEA

Between a man and his wife
nothing ought to rule but love.
WILLIAM PENN (1693)

True love's the gift which God has given
To man alone beneath the heaven:
    It is not fantasy's hot fire,
        Whose wishes, soon as granted, fly;
    It liveth not in fierce desire,
        With dead desire it doth not die;
It is the secret sympathy,
The silver link, the silken tie,
Which heart to heart and mind to mind
In body and in soul can bind.

SIR WALTER SCOTT

True love is always costly.
BILLY GRAHAM

Dear Mary, This is an anniversary letter for you (to make up for the lack of gift). I just wanted to tell you how happy I am with you and with our marriage. I know that neither one of us is perfect (I am certainly not!) and yet the two of us together as a unit comes much closer to perfection than I ever thought possible.

Some days I hardly see you, I must confess, I've grown so accustomed to your face across the table or beside me on the pillow. (But if you were gone, you'd leave an aching hole in my life that would blot out everything.) Other days, I look at you as though I were seeing you for the first time, and I fall in love all over again with this beautiful and fascinating stranger who shares my life.

I love you, Mary. You have helped me be a better man, I do not doubt, a humbler, gentler, happier man. Most of all, you more than any other have helped me see God's face. Like our heavenly Father, you see my strengths; and you know my private weaknesses. You admire my achievements; and you gaze unflinching at my many faults. Either way, your love for me remains, true and reliable, as mysterious to me as grace. How can I doubt God's love, when He has given me yours?

Thank you, my love. Happy Anniversary.

FROM HENRY PRESTON
TO HIS WIFE MARY, 1934

Dear God, thank You that You have revealed Yourself to us in our love for one another. Once again, we give You our love so that You can fill it to the brim with Your Spirit. May it be a vehicle consecrated to You, so that we may not only touch each other with Your love, but also that we may reach out to those around us.

Thank You for sending Christ to be the model of perfect love. Thank You that our own imperfections and weaknesses really don't matter, because we are relying on Your strength and total perfection. Please continue to bless our love. Amen.

I am giving you a new
commandment: Love each other.
Just as I have loved you,
you should love each other.
Your love for one another
will prove to the world
that you are my disciples.

JOHN 13:34–35 (NLT)

1. SAINT SAËNS: The Swan (02:57) *Performed by Klaus Heidlemann and Vladamir Prevost*
2. TCHAIKOVSKY: Andante Cantabile from Op. 11 in 'D' major (06:44) *Performed by the Bel Canto Quartet (Leader Antonio Vezey)*
3. BACH: Prelude in 'C' (02:28) *Performed by Klaus Heidlemann and Sarah Heidlemann*
4. BRAHMS: Wie Melodien (02:17) *Performed by Klaus Heidlemann and Sarah Heidlemann*
5. FAURÉ: Apres un Reve (02:47) *Performed by Klaus Heidlemann and Vladamir Prevost*
6. SCHUMANN: Träumerei (02:27) *Performed by Klaus Heidlemann and Vladamir Prevost*
7. MENDELSSOHN: Andante from Op. 42, No.2 in 'E' minor (06:29) *Performed by the Bel Canto Quartet (Leader Antonio Vezey)*
8. DVORAK: Songs My Mother Taught Me (01:55) *Performed by Klaus Heidlemann and Vladamir Prevost*
9. FAURÉ: Berceuse de Dolly (02:39) *Performed by Klaus Heidlemann and Sarah Heidlemann*
10. MOZART: Andante from K387 in 'G' major (07:22) *Performed by the Bel Canto Quartet (Leader Antonio Vezey)*
11. DEBUSSY: Clair de Lune (04:44) *Performed by Klaus Heidlemann and Sarah Heidlemann*
12. BRAHMS: Romanze from Op. 51, No.1 in 'C' minor (06:45) *Performed by the Bel Canto Quartet (Leader Antonio Vezey)*
13. DEBUSSY: Beau Soir (02:23) *Performed by Klaus Heidlemann and Vladamir Prevost*

TOTAL RUNNING TIME: (52:02)